AF442163

The Periodic Table of Elements

Halogens, Noble Gases and Lanthanides and Actinides

Children's Chemistry Book

BABY PROFESSOR

EDUCATION KIDS

Speedy Publishing LLC
40 E. Main St. #1156
Newark, DE 19711
www.speedypublishing.com

Copyright 2017

All Rights reserved. No part of this book may be reproduced or used in any way or form or by any means whether electronic or mechanical, this means that you cannot record or photocopy any material ideas or tips that are provided in this book

In this book, we're going to briefly cover the Periodic Table of Elements. Then, we're going to take an in-depth look at the Halogens, Noble Gases, and Lanthanides and Actinides, which are groups of elements within the periodic table.

WHAT IS THE PERIODIC TABLE OF ELEMENTS?

The periodic table is a way of organizing all the elements on our planet that scientists have discovered. The number of protons that each element has in its nucleus, which is its atomic number, determines how the elements are organized in rows. Each of the horizontal rows is called a period. The table has either seven or eight periods depending on how you interpret them.

Periodic Table

OF ELEMENTS

1	2	3	4	5	6	7	8	9	10	11	12	13	14	15	16	17	18
H																	He
Li	Be											B	C	N	O	F	Ne
Na	Mg											Al	Si	P	S	Cl	Ar
K	Ca	Sc	Ti	V	Cr	Mn	Fe	Co	Ni	Cu	Zn	Ga	Ge	As	Se	Br	Kr
Rb	Sr	Y	Zr	Nb	Mo	Tc	Ru	Rh	Pd	Ag	Cd	In	Sn	Sb	Te	I	Xe
Cs	Ba	57-71	Hf	Ta	W	Re	Os	Ir	Pt	Au	Hg	Tl	Pb	Bi	Po	At	Rn
Fr	Ra	89-103	Rf	Db	Sg	Bh	Hs	Mt	Ds	Rg	Cn	Uut	Fl	Uup	Lv	Uus	Uuo

Lanthanide Series

La	Ce	Pr	Nd	Pm	Sm	Eu	Gd	Tb	Dy	Ho	Er	Tm	Yb	Lu

Actinide Series

Ac	Th	Pa	U	Np	Pu	Am	Cm	Bk	Cf	Es	Fm	Md	No	Lr

Periodic Table of Elements

METALS

- Alkali Metals
- Alkaline Earth Metals
- Lanthanoids
- Actinoids
- Transition Metals
- Poor Metals

NONMETALS

- Other Nonmetals
- Noble Gases

Li : Solid
Br : Liquid
O : Gas
Sg : Unknown

	1	2	3	4	5	6	7	8	9	10	11	12	13	14	15	16	17	18
A	1 H Hydrogen 1.00794																	2 He Helium 4.002603
B	3 Li Lithium 6.941	4 Be Beryllium 9.012182											5 B Boron 10.811	6 C Carbon 12.0107	7 N Nitrogen 14.0067	8 O Oxygen 15.9994	9 F Fluorine 18.9984032	10 Ne Neon 20.1797
C	11 NA Sodium 22.98976928	12 Mg Magnesium 24.3050											13 Al Aluminium 26.9815386	14 Si Silicon 28.0855	15 P Phosphorus 30.973762	16 S Sulfur 32.065	17 Cl Chlorine 35.453	18 Ar Argon 39.948
D	19 K Potassium 39.0983	20 Ca Calcium 40.078	21 Sc Scandium 44.955912	22 Ti Titanium 47.867	23 V Vanadium 50.9415	24 Cr Chromium 51.9961	25 Mn Manganese 54.938045	26 Fe Iron 55.845	27 Co Cobalt 58.933195	28 Ni Nickel 58.6934	29 Cu Copper 63.546	30 Zn Zinc 65.38	31 Ga Gallium 69.723	32 Ge Germanium 72.64	33 As Arsenic 74.92160	34 Se Selenium 78.96	35 Br Bromine 79.904	36 Kr Krypton 83.798
E	37 Rb Rubidium 85.4678	38 Sr Strontium 87.62	39 Y Yttrium 88.90585	40 Zr Zirconium 91.224	41 Nb Niobium 92.90638	42 Mo Molybdenum 95.96	43 Tc Technetium (97.9072)	44 Ru Ruthenium 101.07	45 Rh Rhodium 102.90550	46 Pd Palladium 106.42	47 Ag Silver 107.8682	48 Cd Cadmium 112.411	49 In Indium 114.818	50 Sn Tin 118.710	51 Sb Antimony 121.760	52 Te Tellurium 127.60	53 I Iodine 126.90447	54 Xe Xenon 131.293
F	55 Cs Caesium 132.9054519	56 Ba Barium 137.327	57-71	72 Hf Hafnium 178.49	73 Ta Tantalum 180.94788	74 W Tungsten 183.84	75 Re Rhenium 186.207	76 Os Osmium 190.23	77 Ir Iridium 192.217	78 Pt Platinum 195.084	79 Au Gold 196.966569	80 Hg Mercury 200.59	81 Tl Thallium 204.3833	82 Pb Lead 207.2	83 Bi Bismuth 208.98040	84 Po Polonium (208.9824)	85 At Astatine (209.9871)	86 Rn Radon (222.0176)
G	87 Fr Francium (223)	88 Ra Radium (226)	89-103	104 Rf Rutherfordium (261)	105 Db Dubnium (262)	106 Sg Seaborgium (266)	107 Bh Bohrium (264)	108 Hs Hassium (277)	109 Mt Meitnerium (268)	110 Ds Darmstadtium (271)	111 Rg Roentgenium (272)	112 Uub Ununtrium (285)	113 Uut Ununtrium (284)	114 Uuq Ununquadium (289)	115 Uup Ununpentium (288)	116 Uuh Ununhexium (292)	117 Uus Ununseptium	118 Uuo Ununoctium (294)

57 La Lanthanum 138.90547	58 Ce Cerium 140.116	59 Pr Praseodymium 140.90765	60 Nd Neodymium 144.242	61 Pm Promethium (145)	62 Sm Samarium 150.36	63 Eu Europium 151.25	64 Gd Gadolinium 157.25	65 Tb Terbium 158.92535	66 Dy Dysprosium 162.500	67 Ho Holmium 164.93032	68 Er Erbium 167.259	69 Tm Thulium 168.93421	70 Yb Ytterbium 173.054	71 Lu Lutetium 174.9668
89 Ac Actinium (227)	90 Th Thorium 232.03806	91 Pa Protactinium 231.03588	92 U Uranium 238.02891	93 Np Neptunium (237)	94 Pu Plutonium (244)	95 Am Americium (243)	96 Cm Curium (247)	97 Bk Berkelium (247)	98 Cf Californium (251)	99 Es Einsteinium (252)	100 Fm Fermium (257)	101 Md Mendelevium (258)	102 No Nobelium (259)	103 Lr Lawrencium (262)

The elements of hydrogen and helium make up the first short period of just 2 elements while the sixth period has 32 elements. As you move across a period or row and travel from left to right, the element at the leftmost edge of the table has only 1 electron in its outer shell, while the element at the rightmost edge has a full shell of electrons.

WHY ARE THE COLUMNS IN THE PERIODIC TABLE IMPORTANT?

Just like the rows in the table are important, the columns are important as well.

Periodic Table of Elements

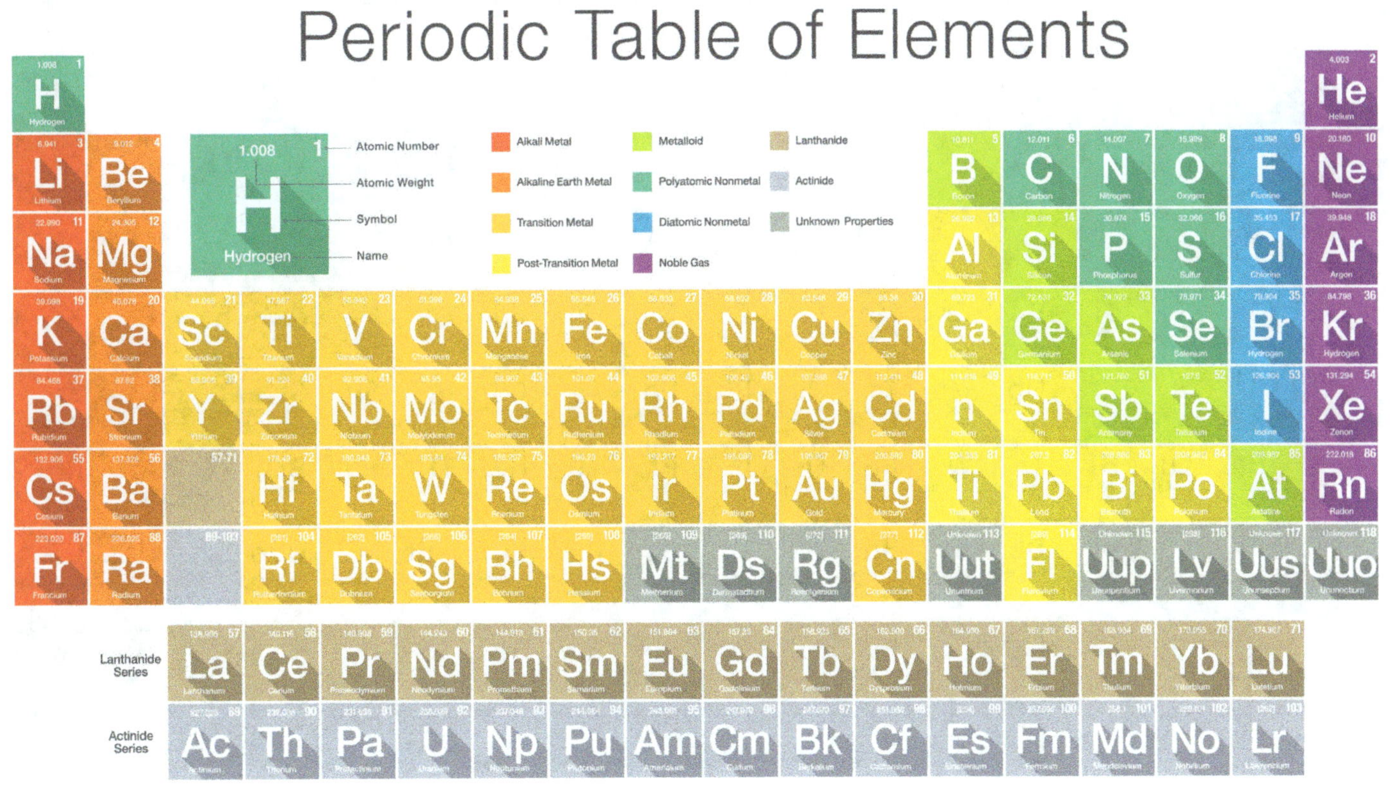

The Periodic Table of the Elements

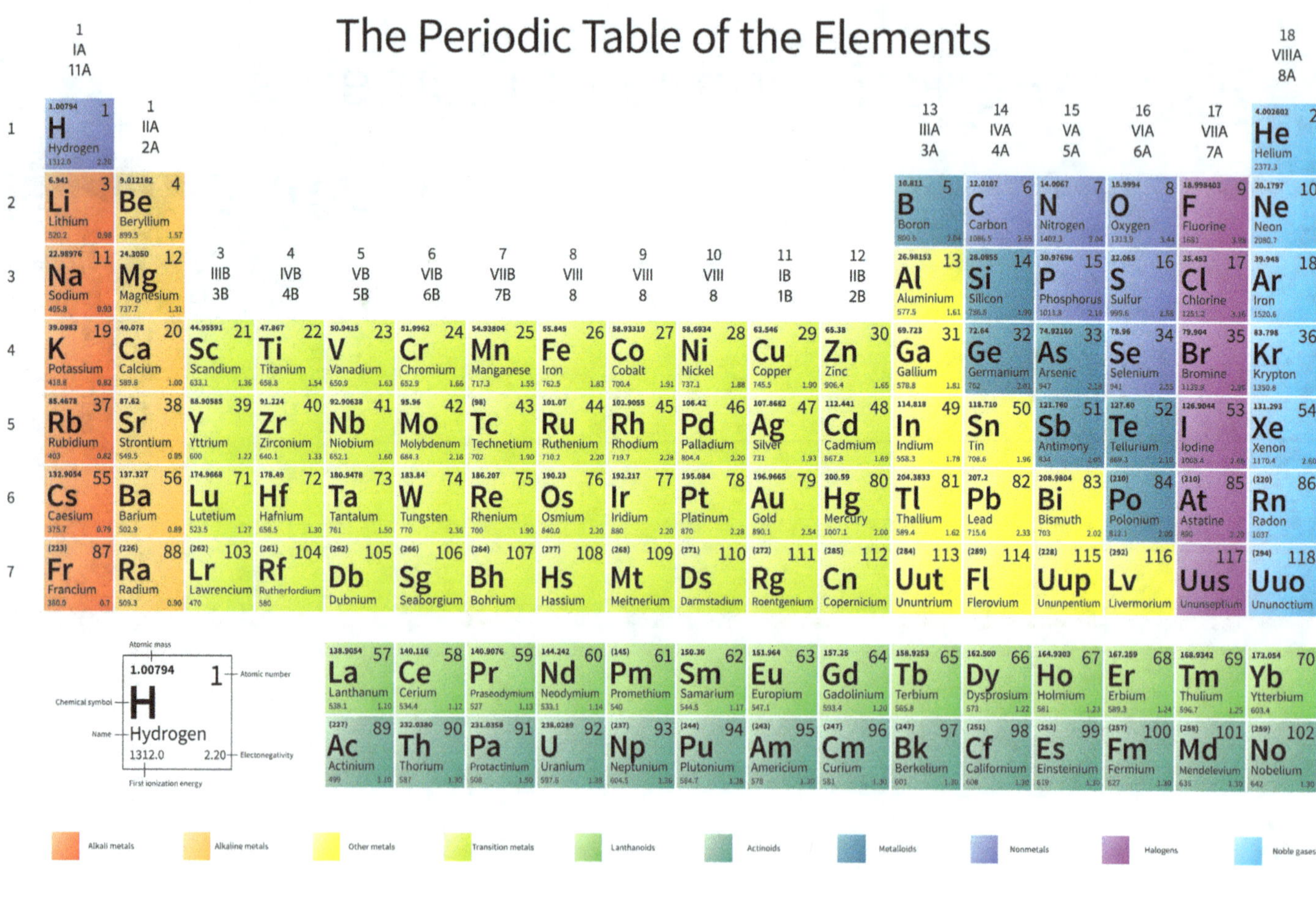

There are 18 groups within the table and each group has its own set of properties. By studying the way the groups are organized, chemists can make predictions about the behavior and chemical properties of certain elements.

ABBREVIATIONS IN THE PERIODIC TABLE

The periodic table contains abbreviations for all the names of the elements. Sometimes these abbreviations are easy to figure out and sometimes they're not.

PERIODIC TABLE OF THE ELEMENTS
Long Shadow Style

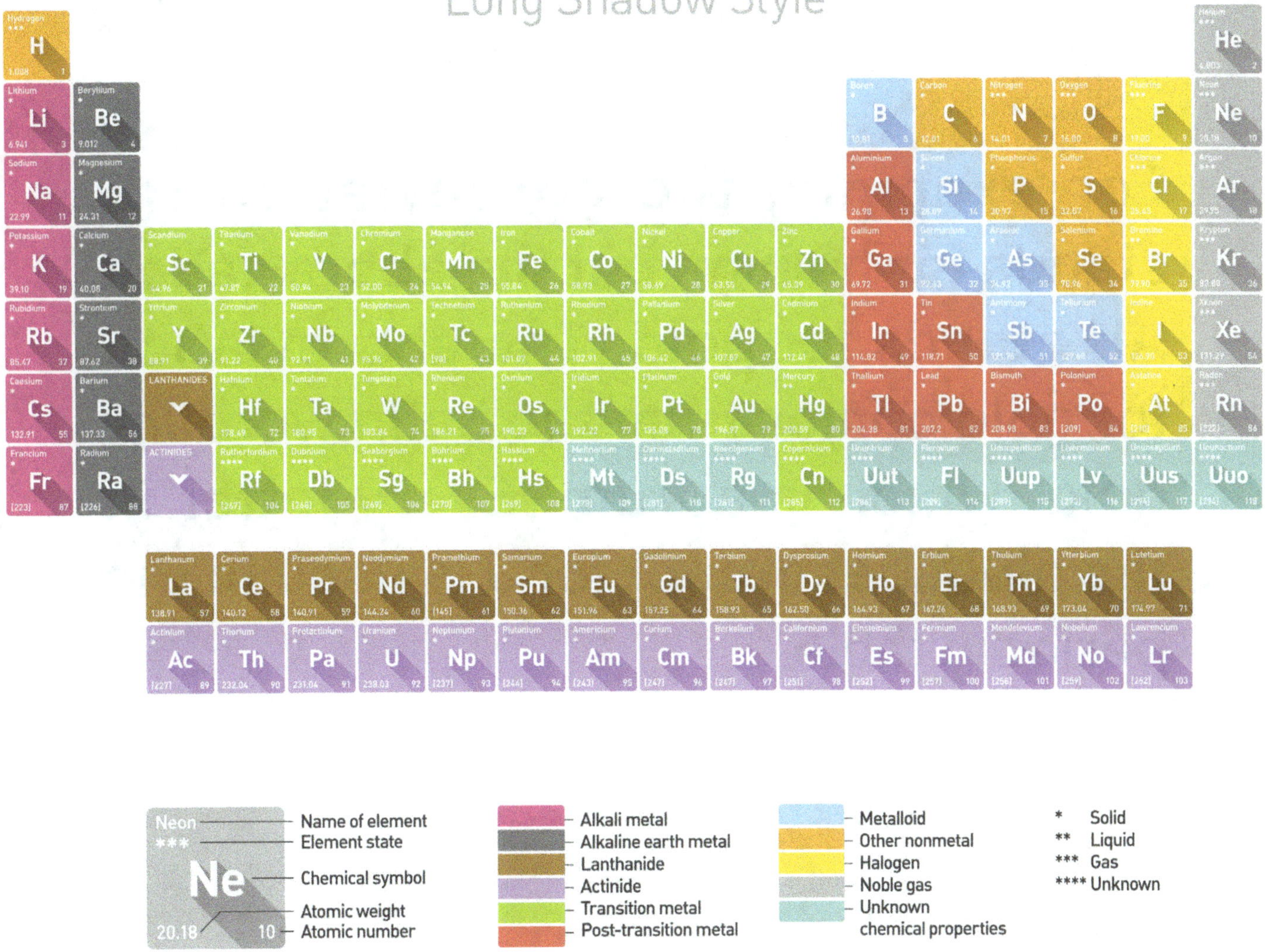

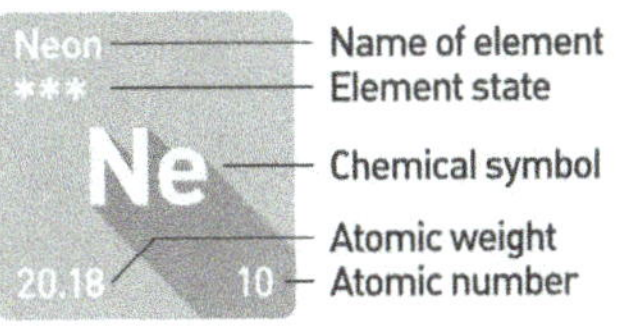

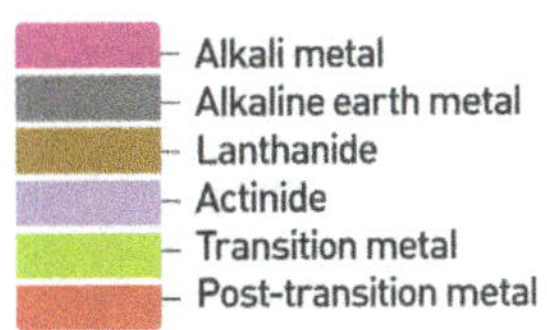

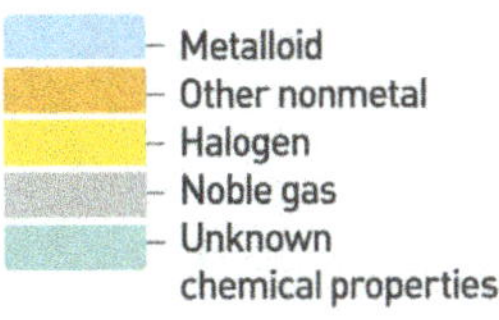

For example, the abbreviation HE stands for helium, but the abbreviation AU stands for gold. The abbreviation for gold comes from the Latin word for gold, which is aurum. Every letter in the alphabet except for J is used in the periodic table.

★★ Periodic Table Of The Elements ★★

GROUP / **PERIOD**

| | 1a | 2a | 3b | 4b | 5b | 6b | 7b | 8 | 8 | 8 | 1b | 2b | 3a | 4a | 5a | 6a | 7a | 0 |

Metals
- Alkali Metals
- Alkaline Earth Metals
- Actinoids
- Lanthanoids
- Transition Metals
- Poor Metals

Nonmetals
- Other Nonmetals
- Noble Gases

Period 1
- 1 H Hydrogen 1.00794
- 2 He Helium 4.0026

Period 2
- 3 Li Lithium 6.941
- 4 Be Beryllium 9.0122
- 5 B Boron 10.811
- 6 C Carbon 12.011
- 7 N Nitrogen 14.0067
- 8 O Oxygen 15.9994
- 9 F Fluorine 18.9984
- 10 Ne Neon 20.183

Period 3
- 11 Na Sodium 22.9893
- 12 Mg Magnesium 24.305
- 13 Al Aluminium 26.9815
- 14 Si Silicon 28.086
- 15 P Phosphorus 30.9738
- 16 S Sulfur 32.064
- 17 Cl Chlorine 35.453
- 18 Ar Argon 39.948

Period 4
- 19 K Potassium 39.098
- 20 Ca Calcium 40.08
- 21 Sc Scandium 44.956
- 22 Ti Titanium 47.87
- 23 V Vanadium 50.942
- 24 Cr Chromium 51.996
- 25 Mn Manganese 54.9380
- 26 Fe Iron 55.845
- 27 Co Cobalt 58.9332
- 28 Ni Nickel 58.69
- 29 Cu Copper 63.546
- 30 Zn Zinc 65.39
- 31 Ga Gallium 69.72
- 32 Ge Germanium 72.61
- 33 As Arsenic 74.9216
- 34 Se Selenium 78.96
- 35 Br Bromine 79.904
- 36 Kr Krypton 83.80

Period 5
- 37 Rb Rubidium 85.47
- 38 Sr Strontium 87.62
- 39 Y Yttrium 88.906
- 40 Zr Zirconium 91.22
- 41 Nb Niobium 92.906
- 42 Mo Molybdenum 95.94
- 43 Tc Technetium (98)
- 44 Ru Ruthenium 101.07
- 45 Rh Rhodium 102.905
- 46 Pd Palladium 106.4
- 47 Ag Silver 107.868
- 48 Cd Cadmium 112.41
- 49 In Indium 114.82
- 50 Sn Tin 118.71
- 51 Sb Antimony 121.76
- 52 Te Tellurium 127.60
- 53 I Iodine 126.9045
- 54 Xe Xenon 131.29

Period 6
- 55 Cs Cesium 132.905
- 56 Ba Barium 137.33
- 72 Hf Hafnium 178.49
- 73 Ta Tantalum 180.948
- 74 W Tungsten 183.84
- 75 Re Rhenium 186.2
- 76 Os Osmium 190.2
- 77 Ir Iridium 192.2
- 78 Pt Platinum 195.08
- 79 Au Gold 196.967
- 80 Hg Mercury 200.59
- 81 Tl Thallium 204.38
- 82 Pb Lead 207.2
- 83 Bi Bismuth 208.98
- 84 Po Polonium (210)
- 85 At Astatine (210)
- 86 Rn Radon (222)

Period 7
- 87 Fr Francium (223)
- 88 Ra Radium (226)
- 89–103** Actinides
- 104 Rf Rutherfordium (261)
- 105 Db Dubnium (261)
- 106 Sg Seaborgium (264)
- 107 Bh Bohrium (264)
- 108 Hs Hassium (265)
- 109 Mt Meitnerium (268)
- 110 Ds Darmstadtium (281)
- 111 Rg Roentgenium (280)
- 112 (277)

Lanthanides
- La, Ce, Pr, Nd, Pm, Sm, Eu, Gd, Tb, Dy, Ho, Er, Tm, Yb, Lu

****ACTINIDES**
- 89 Ac Actinium (227)
- 90 Th Thorium 232.038
- 91 Pa Protactinium 231.036
- 92 U Uranium 238.02
- 93 Np Neptunium (237)
- 94 Pu Plutonium (244)
- 95 Am Americium (243)
- 96 Cm Curium (247)
- 97 Bk Berkelium (247)
- 98 Cf Californium (251)
- 99 Es Einsteinium (252)
- 100 Fm Fermium (257)
- 101 Md Mendelevium (258)
- 102 No Nobelium (259)
- 103 Lr Lawrencium (262)

fluorine

F

9

chlorine

Cl

17

bromine

Br

35

iodine

I

53

astatine

At

85

WHAT ARE HALOGENS?

In the second column from the right side of the periodic table, in column 17, are elements in a group called the halogens. They are positioned to the left of the noble gases and right of the group called "other nonmetals." There are five elements in this group and their names all end in "ine." They are astatine, bromine, chlorine, fluorine, and iodine.

WHAT PROPERTIES MAKE HALOGENS SIMILAR?

In their outer shells, all of the halogens have seven valence electrons. They are just one electron short of having full shells and this means they are very reactive.

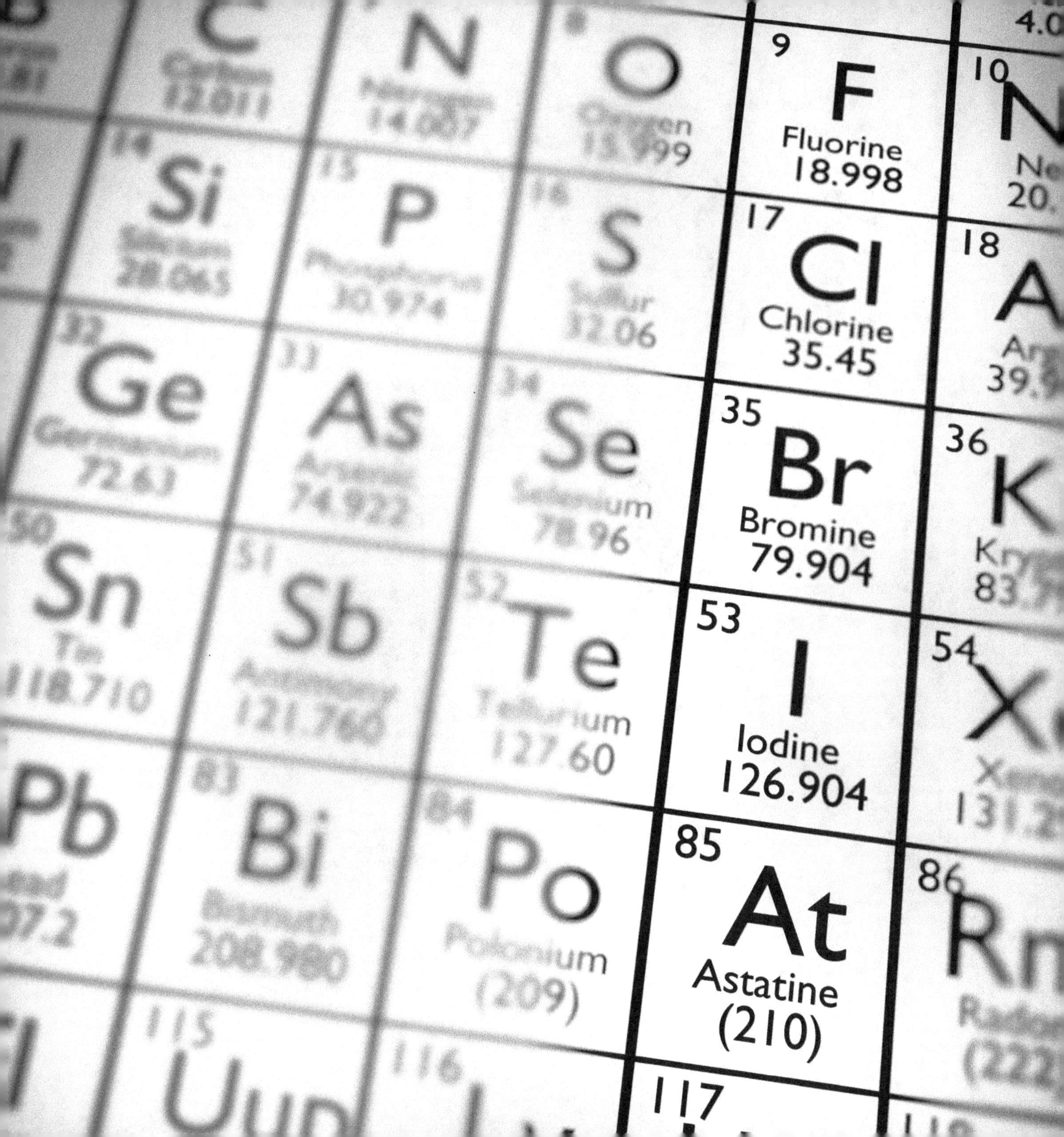

C
N
O
9 F Fluorine 18.998
10 Ne 20.
Si 28.085
15 P 30.974
16 S 32.06
17 Cl Chlorine 35.45
18 Ar 39.9
Ge 72.63
33 As 74.922
34 Se 78.96
35 Br Bromine 79.904
36 Kr 83.
Sn 118.710
51 Sb 121.760
52 Te Tellurium 127.60
53 I Iodine 126.904
54 X
Pb 207.2
83 Bi 208.980
84 Po Polonium (209)
85 At Astatine (210)
86 Rn
115
116
117
4.0

17

35.453

Cl

Chlorine

Reactive just means that they frequently bond with other elements. Fluorine is the most reactive of the halogen elements and it combines readily with most of the elements.

As you move down a column in the table, the elements get less and less reactive. The chemical properties of an element are slightly different than the properties of the element that appears above it in the table. Another similarity these elements have is that they all create acids when they are joined with hydrogen.

OF ELEMENTS
18
VIIIA
ATOMIC NUMBER
SYMBOL
NAME
0
15
VA
Fluorine
18.998
17
-2
+4
+6
-1
+1
+3
+5
+7
18
Cl
Chlorine
35.453
35
-1
+1
51
+3
+5
Sb
Antimony
121.76
Tellurium
127.6
131.29
83
+2
+4
+3
+5
84
+2
+4
85
86
0
Bi
Po
At
Rn
74.92
STA
GA

The word "halogen" comes from the Greek words that mean "to make salt." All five halogens easily form salt compounds. In fact, many of the salts in seawater are compounds that consist of a halogen combined with a metal element. An example of this is the compound magnesium chloride. The table salt that we use everyday in our food is sodium chloride, another such compound.

Another common characteristic of the halogens is that they have a strong odor. The element of bromine gets its name from the Greek word for "stench."

9

fluorum

$2s^2 2p^5$

18,9984

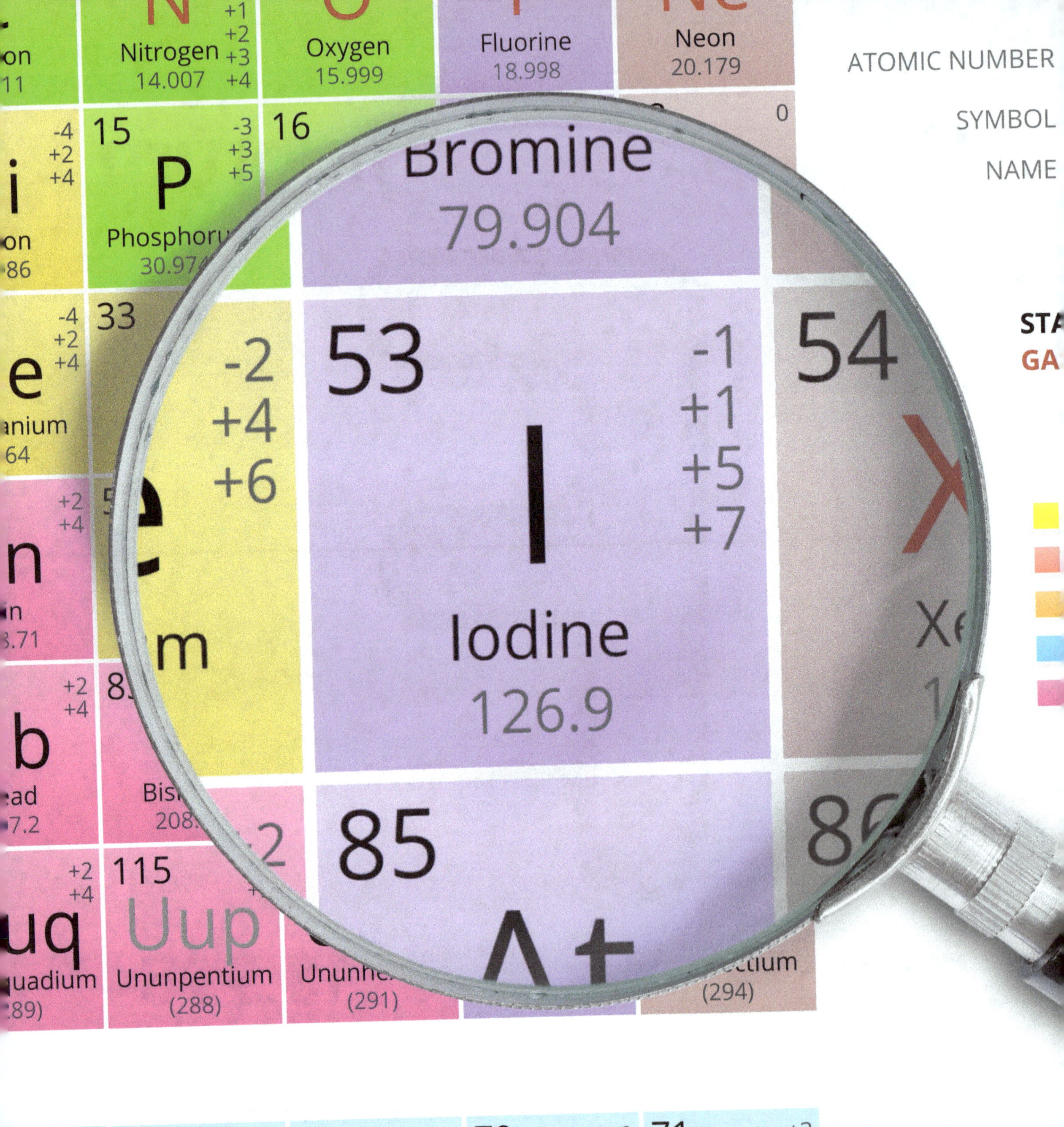

Nitrogen
14.007
Oxygen
15.999
Fluorine
18.998
Neon
20.179
ATOMIC NUMBER
SYMBOL
NAME
15
P
Phosphoru
30.97
-3
+3
+5
16
Bromine
79.904
53
-2
+4
+6
-1
+1
+5
+7
54
I
Iodine
126.9
33
85
115
Uup
Ununpentium
(288)
Ununhe
(291)
(294)

All the halogen elements have diatomic molecules, which simply means that in their natural form their molecules are made up of two atoms.

THE FORM OF HALOGENS IN STANDARD CONDITIONS

The halogen elements, under regular conditions, show up as all three of the types of matter. The elements of fluorine and chlorine are gases, the element of iodine and the element of astatine are solids, and then there's bromine, which is a liquid. The only element other than bromine that is a liquid in its natural state at around 70 degrees Fahrenheit is the element of mercury.

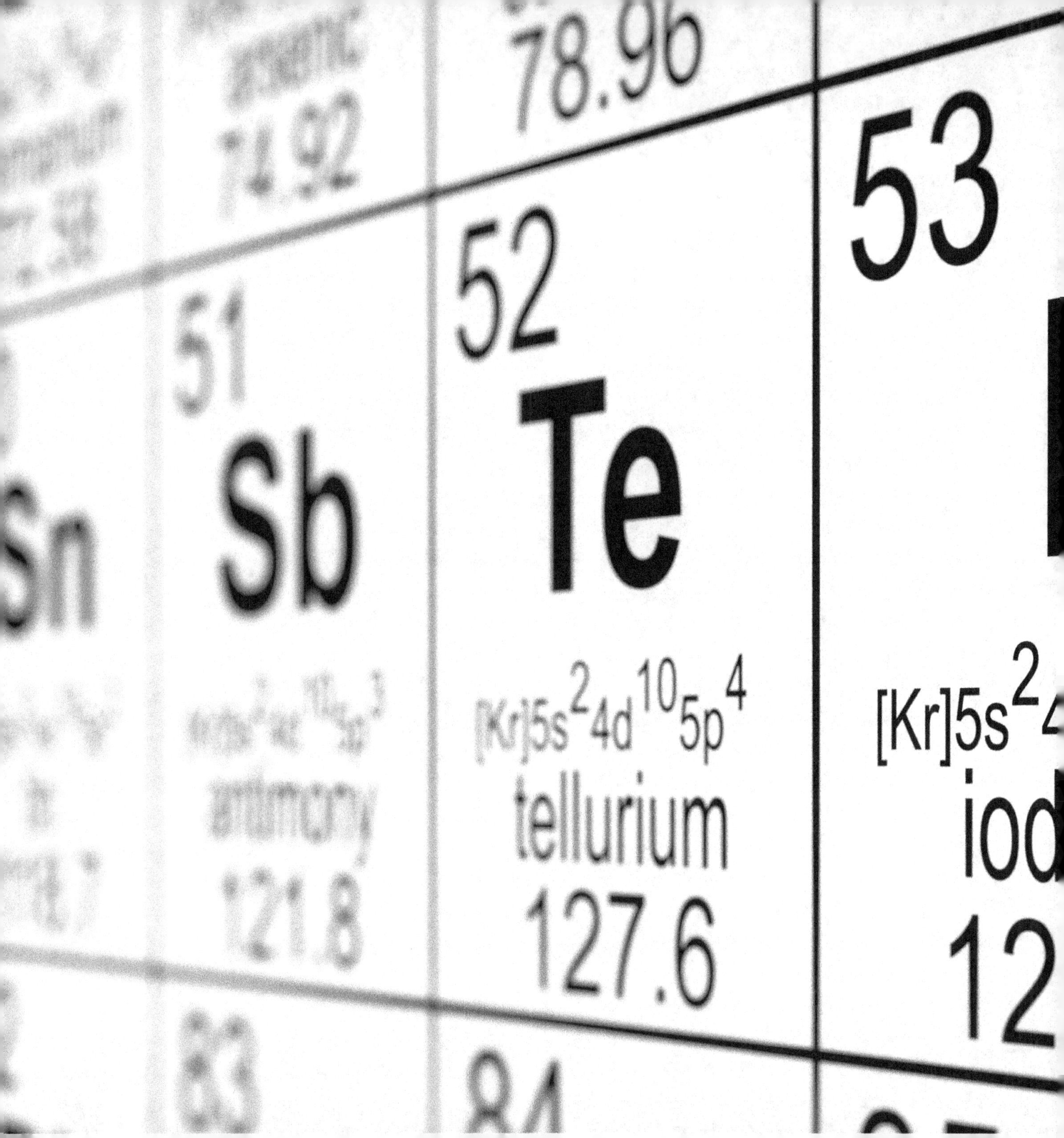
74.92
78.96
53
51
Sb
52
Te
[Kr]5s²4d¹⁰5p⁴
tellurium
127.6
antimony
121.8
Sn
[Kr]5s²4
iod
83
84
12

FLUORINE
9
F
18.998

The Earth's crust contains all five halogens with fluorine being the most abundant and astatine being the most rare.

FASCINATING FACTS ABOUT HALOGENS AND HALIDES

• Halogen light bulbs contain iodine and bromine. They give off brighter light than regular electric light bulbs. They're frequently used to flood stadiums with light at nighttime.

• Fluorine is so deadly that taking in air that contains 0.1% of it causes death.

• Salts made with chlorine are used for swimming pool water to kill germs.

• When a halogen reacts with and combines with another element, the simple compound that is formed is called a halide. A common example that you know about is table salt, which is sodium chloride. Another that you may have heard of, is fluoride, which is often added to drinking water to help us prevent tooth decay.

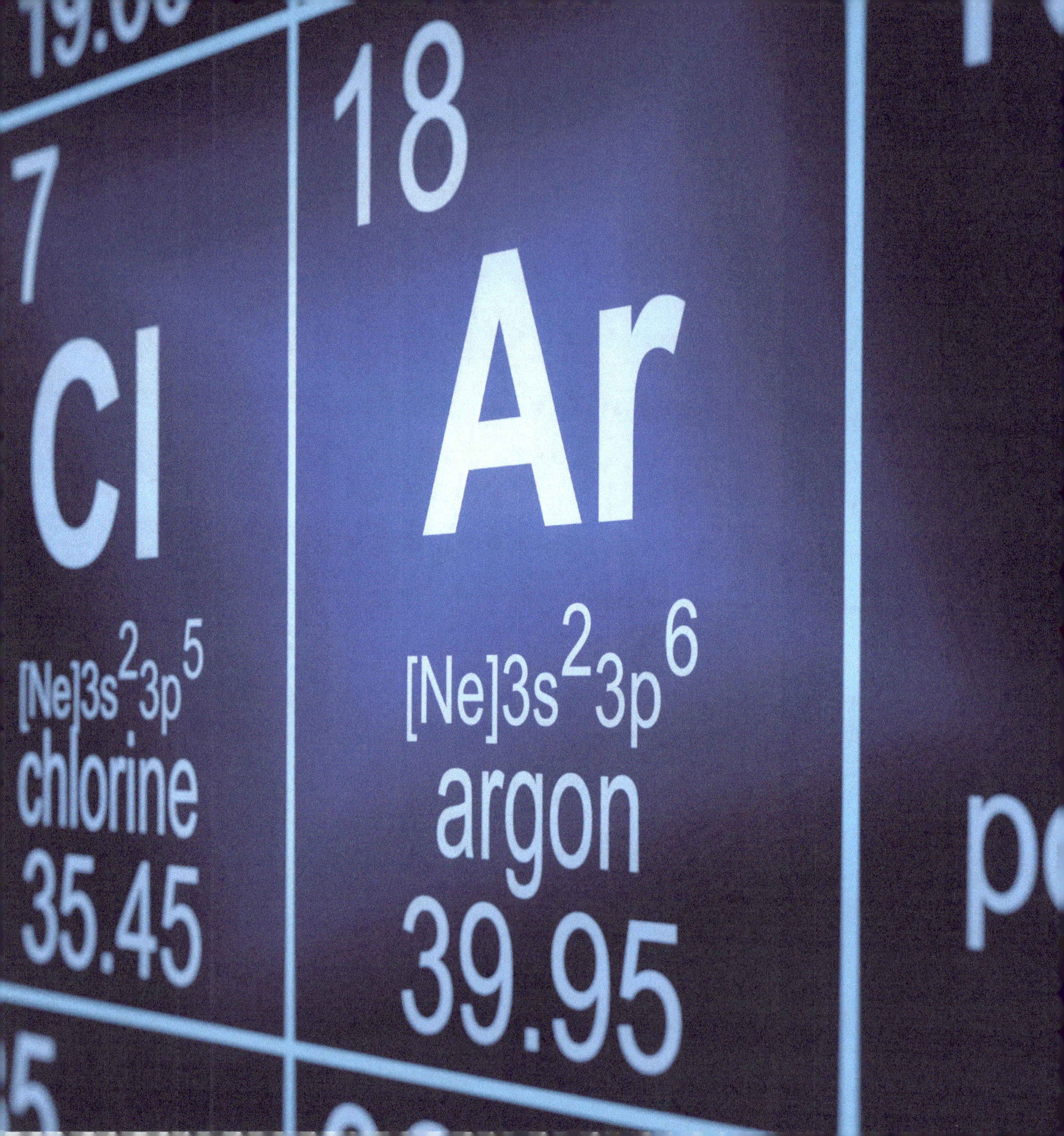

7

18

Cl

Ar

[Ne]3s^{2}3p^5

[Ne]3s^{2}3p^6

chlorine

argon

35.45

39.95

WHAT ARE THE NOBLE GASES?

The noble gases are located in the rightmost column of the periodic table, column 18. These elements, also called the inert gases, have a full outer shell of eight electrons except for helium, which has a full shell with only two electrons.

Because of these full shells, they very rarely combine. They are non-reactive and are also called the "inert" gases because of this characteristic. There are six noble gases. They are argon, helium, krypton, neon, radon, and xenon.

18
VIIIA
2
4.0026
He
HELIUM
IIIA
98
10
20.180

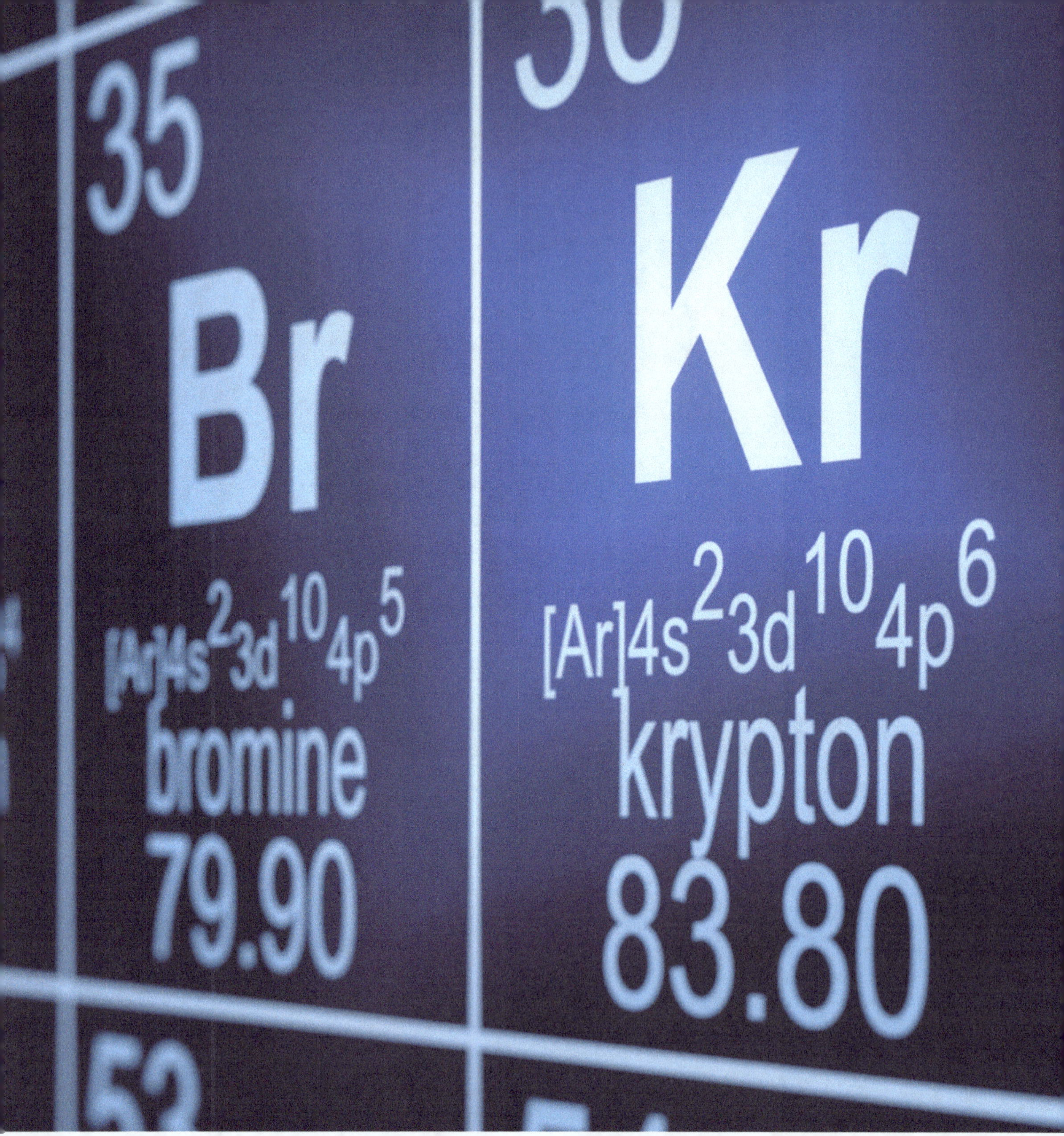

35	36
Br	**Kr**
$[Ar]4s^2 3d^{10} 4p^5$	$[Ar]4s^2 3d^{10} 4p^6$
bromine	krypton
79.90	83.80

53

WHAT PROPERTIES MAKE NOBLE GASES SIMILAR?

Since they have full outer shells, the elements of the noble gases are very stable. Because of this, they are often used in laboratory experiments where reactions need to be slowed down. Under standard conditions, they are colorless and odorless gases. They have a very narrow range where they can form liquids because their temperatures for melting and boiling are so close together.

CAN NOBLE GASES FORM BONDS?

About 40 years ago, scientists discovered that they could force the noble gases to form bonds. Some of these compounds have been used to create explosives. Under most natural conditions, the noble gases don't react with other elements.

10
Ne
Neon
20.1797

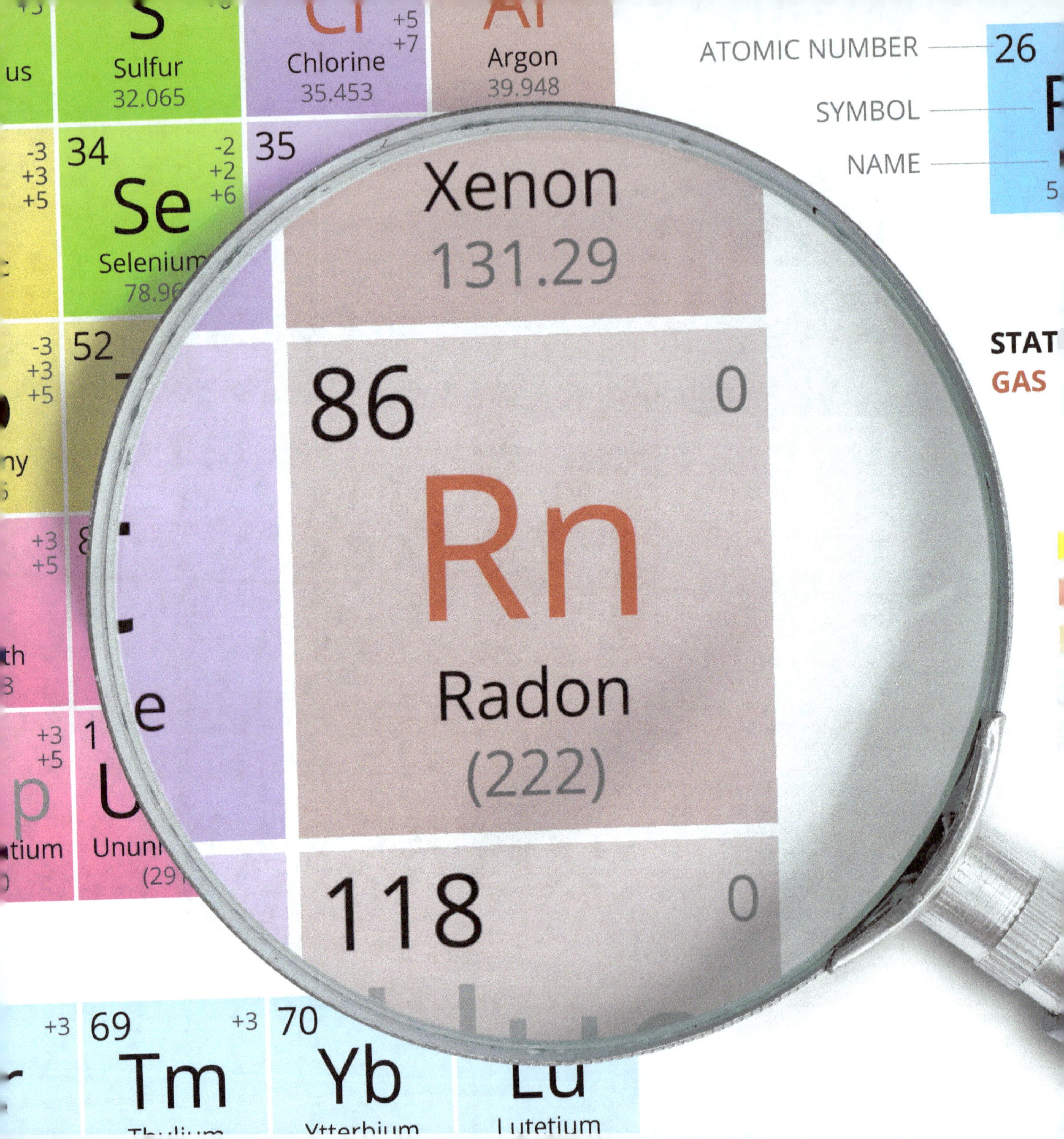
Sulfur
32.065
Chlorine
35.453
+5
+7
Argon
39.948
34
-3
+3
+5
Se
Selenium
78.96
-2
+2
+6
35
52
-3
+3
+5
+3
+5
+3
+5
Ununn
(29
69
+3
Tm
70
+3
Yb
Lu
Xenon
131.29
86
0
Rn
Radon
(222)
118
0
ATOMIC NUMBER
26
SYMBOL
NAME
STAT
GAS

HOW ABUNDANT ARE THE NOBLE GASES?

On Earth, the noble gases are rare except for the element of argon, which makes up about 1% of our planet's atmosphere. It's the third most dominant gas in our atmosphere after the elements of nitrogen and oxygen.

However, throughout the universe, the abundance of the noble gases is a different story. The element of helium makes up about one-fourth of the mass of all elements in the known universe.

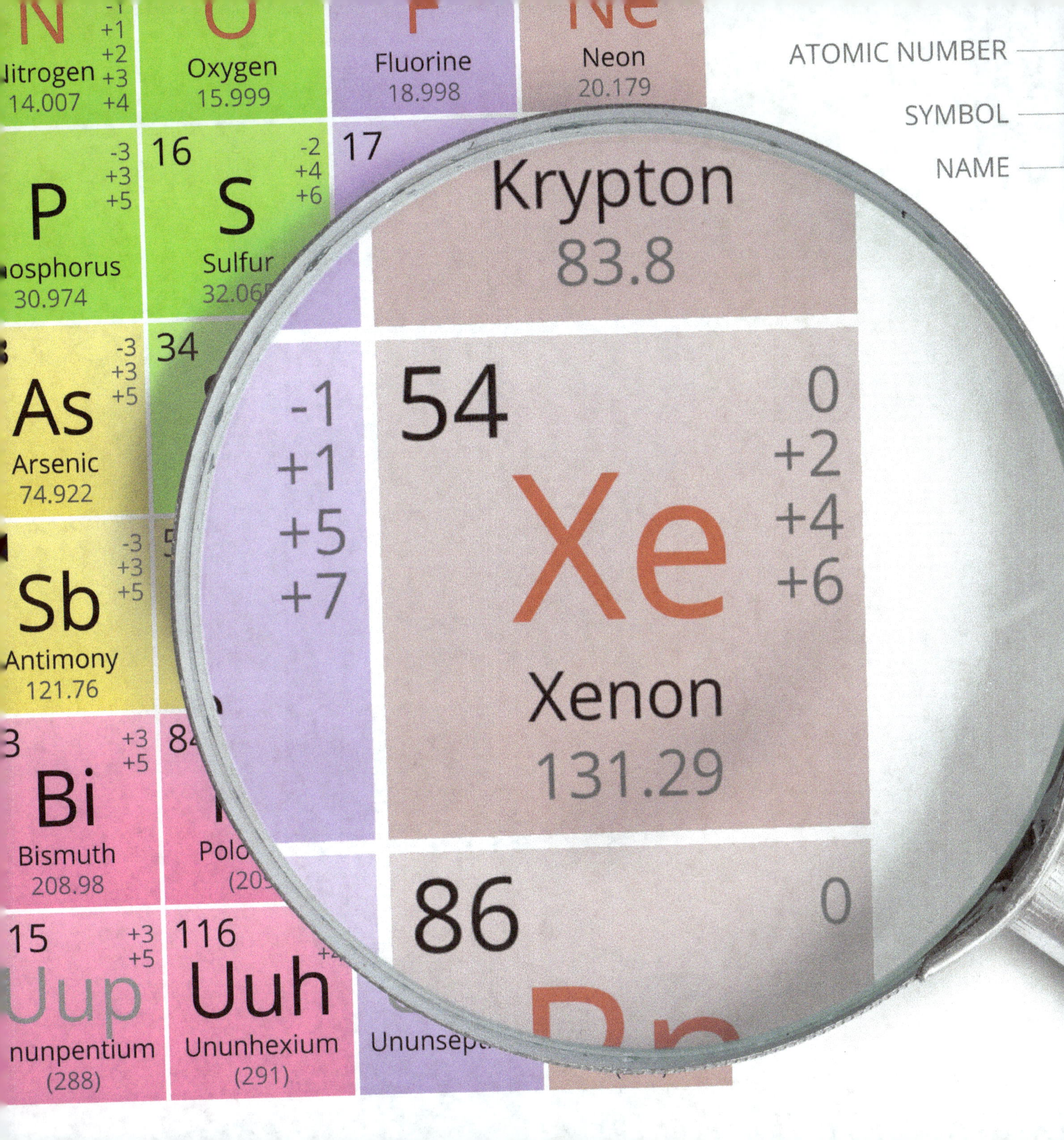

N
Nitrogen
14.007
-1
+1
+2
+3
+4
Oxygen
15.999
Fluorine
18.998
Ne
Neon
20.179
ATOMIC NUMBER
SYMBOL
NAME
P
-3
+3
+5
16
osphorus
30.974
S
Sulfur
32.06
-2
+4
+6
17
Krypton
83.8
As
-3
+3
+5
34
Arsenic
74.922
-1
+1
+5
+7
54
0
+2
+4
+6
Xe
Xenon
131.29
Sb
-3
+3
+5
Antimony
121.76
Bi
+3
+5
84
Bismuth
208.98
Polo
(20
86
0
15
+3
+5
Uup
nunpentium
(288)
116
Uuh
Ununhexium
(291)
Ununsept

INTERESTING FACTS ABOUT NOBLE, ALSO CALLED INERT, GASES

- Because it is stable and non-flammable, helium is a much safer gas to use in balloons than hydrogen is.

- The element of krypton was named after the Greek word "kryptos," which translates to "the hidden one."

- Sir William Ramsay, the Scottish chemist, discovered many of these gases.

- With the exception of radon, all the noble gases have isotopes that are stable.

- When you hear neon, you may think of neon signs, but neon signs are made of a mixture of the noble gases and other elements to achieve their bright lights in varying colors.

- The element of xenon was named after the Greek word "xenos," which means "foreigner."

WHAT ARE THE LANTHANIDES AND ACTINIDES?

The group of elements called lanthanides and the group called actinides are listed below the main part of the periodic table. There are 30 elements in both groups together and they are often called the "inner transition metals."

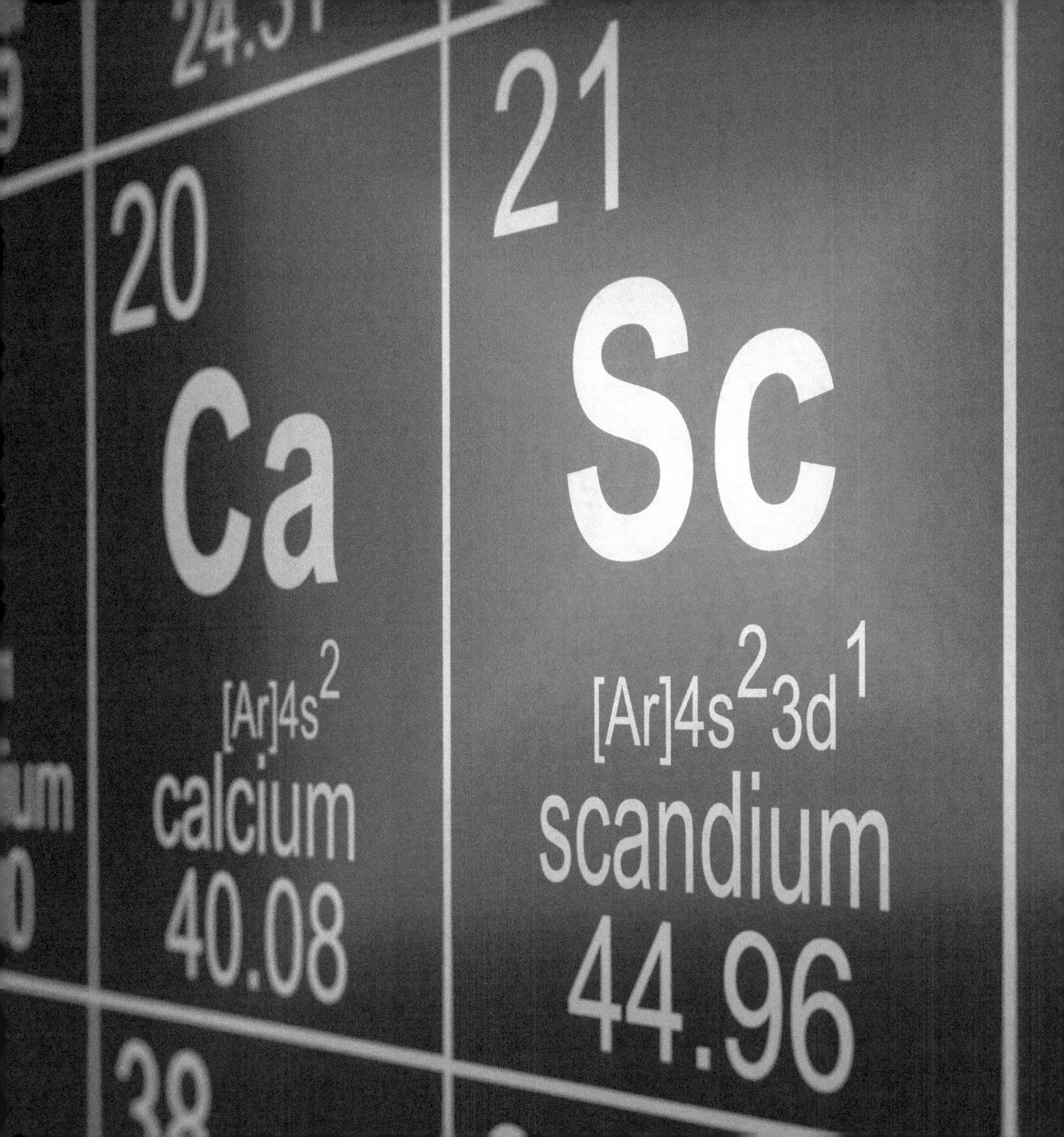

24.31
20
Ca
$[Ar]4s^2$
calcium
40.08
21
Sc
$[Ar]4s^2 3d^1$
scandium
44.96
38

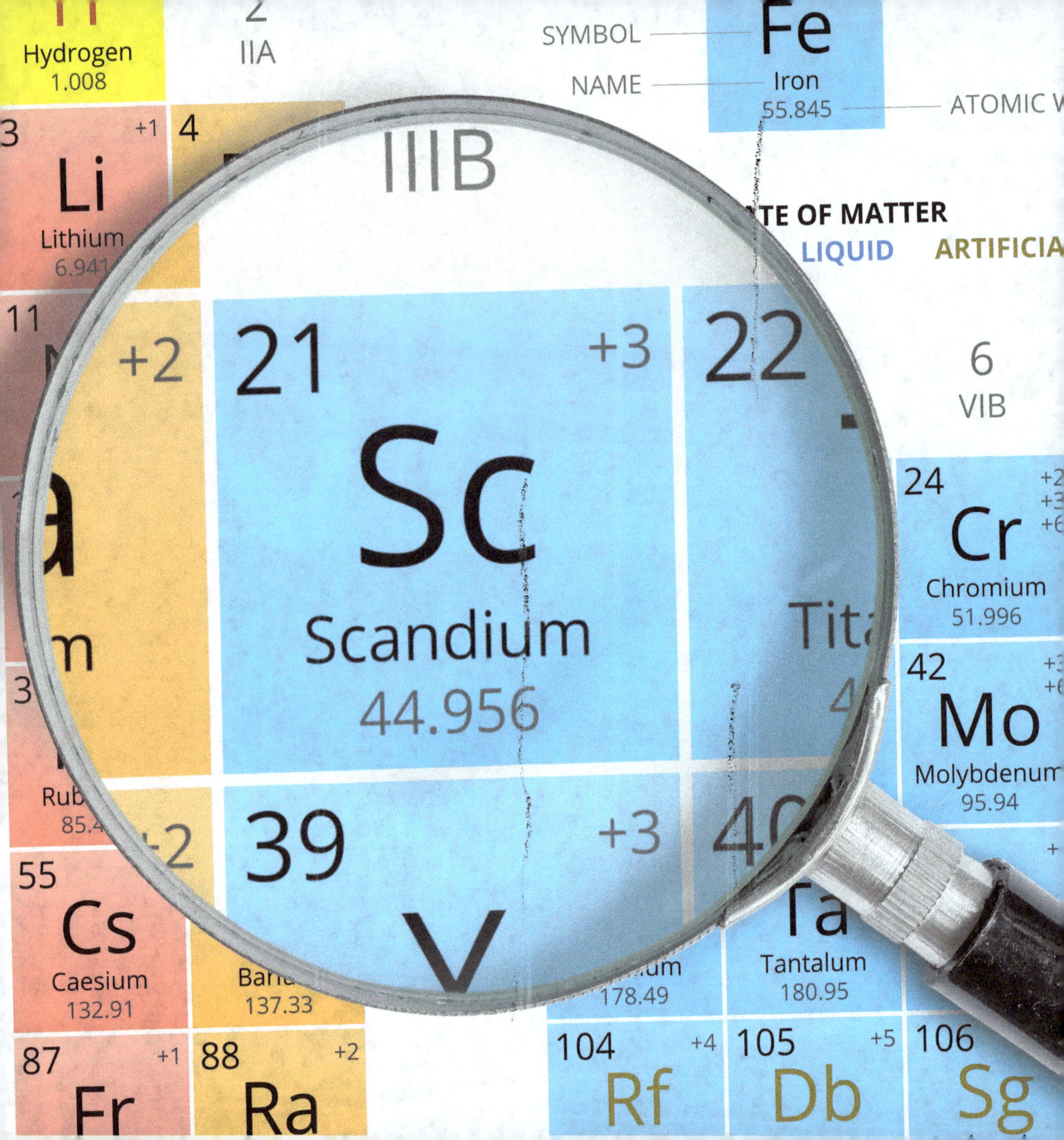
Hydrogen
1.008
IIA
IIIB
SYMBOL
Fe
NAME
Iron
55.845
ATOMIC W
TE OF MATTER
LIQUID
ARTIFICIA
3
+1
Li
Lithium
6.941
4
11
+2
21
+3
Sc
Scandium
44.956
22
6
VIB
24
+2
+3
+6
Cr
Chromium
51.996
42
Mo
Molybdenum
95.94
Rub
85.4
3
39
+3
40
V
Tita
55
Cs
Caesium
132.91
Bari
137.33
178.49
Ta
Tantalum
180.95
87
+1
Fr
88
+2
Ra
104
+4
Rf
105
+5
Db
106
Sg

Their atomic numbers are in the range of 57 to 71. This group of 15 total metals is named after lanthanum since all the elements in this group have similar characteristics to this element. Along with the elements of scandium and yttrium, the lanthanides are considered to be rare.

One of the characteristics that the lanthanides share is that they are metal elements, usually silver-white in color, and they are frequently found in ores.

58
Ce
Cerium
140.116
[Xe]4f5d6s 2
5.5387
D 3/2
La
Lanthanum
138.9055
[Xe]5d6s 2
5.5769
2D 3/2
90
Th
89
Ac

138.91
Ce
140.12
actinium
89
Ac
[227]
thorium
90
Th
232.

Just as the lanthanides are named after the element lanthanum, actinides are named after their first element, which is actinium. The actinide group is primarily made up of elements that are man-made, but there are a few elements that occur naturally such as thorium and uranium. There are also 15 elements in this group and their atomic numbers range from 89 to 103.

FASCINATING FACTS ABOUT LANTHANIDES AND ACTINIDES

- The elements of uranium and plutonium, which are from the actinide group, are well-known since they are used in nuclear bombs.

- Hybrid cars and magnets that are permanent as well as superconductors all use elements in the lanthanide group.

- When an element has an atomic number greater than the atomic number of 92, the number of uranium, then it is called "transuranium." Many transuranium elements are made in laboratory conditions inside nuclear reactors.

- Both groups are highly reactive when combined with halogens.

- The word "actinides" comes from the Greek word "aktis," which means ray or beam. Uranium was one of the first actinides discovered.

Periodic Table of Elements

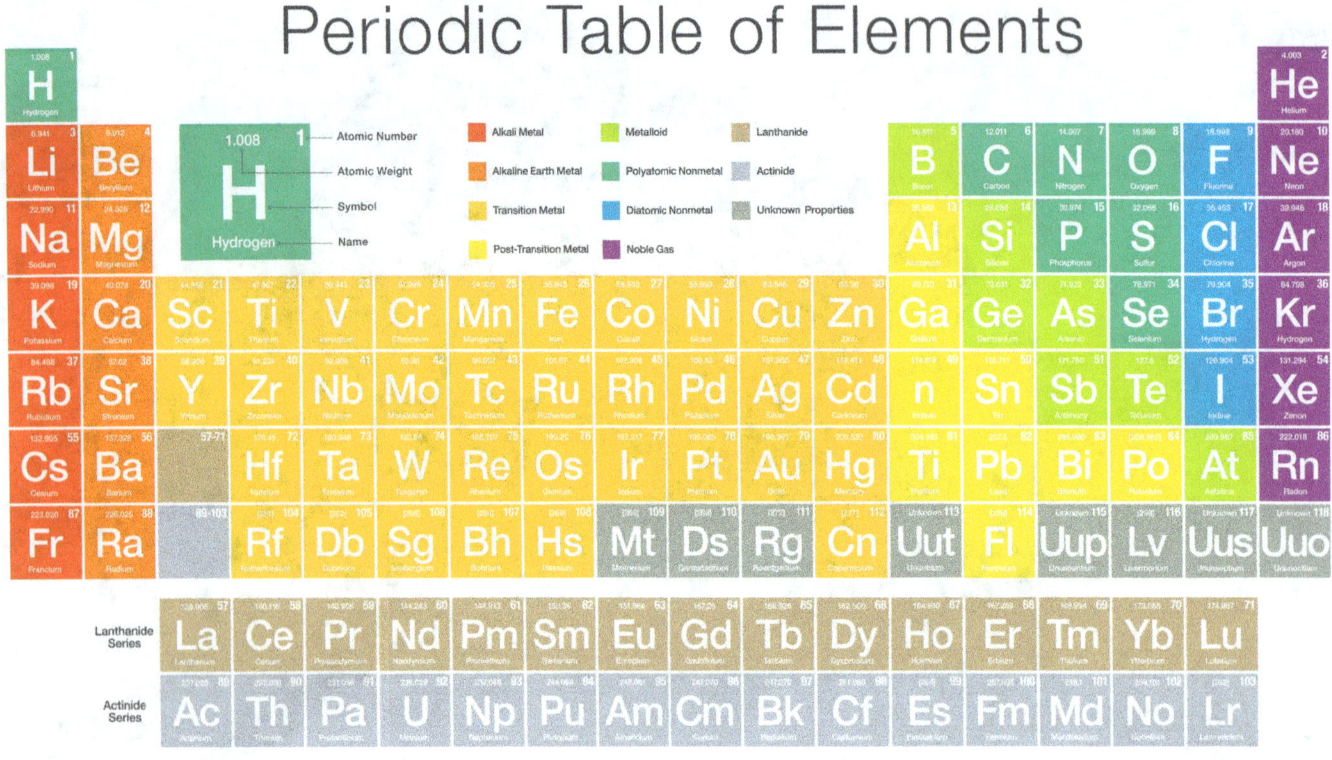

Awesome! Now that you've read this book you know more about Chemistry and the Periodic Table including the halogens and the noble gases. You also learned about the lanthanides and actinides. You can find more Chemistry books from Baby Professor by searching the website of your favorite book retailer.

Visit
BABY PROFESSOR
EDUCATION KIDS
www.BabyProfessorBooks.com
to download Free Baby Professor eBooks
and view our catalog of new and exciting
Children's Books

www.ingramcontent.com/pod-product-compliance
Lightning Source LLC
Chambersburg PA
CBHW081147180726
48003CB00026B/2905